Will our children

EVERY CHILD ..SO
IS A GENIUS... THE
ARE
TO ▪▪▪▪▪▪
OUT!

CHiLDREN
FEELiNG
GOOD

Tony Humphreys BA, HDE, MA, PhD

VERITAS

First published 1998 by
Veritas Publications
7/8 Lower Abbey Street
Dublin 1

ISBN 1 85390 374 4

Design: Bill Bolger
Cover illustration: Angela Hampton Family Life Pictures
© Angela Hampton
Cartoons: John Byrne
Printed in Ireland by Betaprint Ltd, Dublin

CONTENTS

1. Children receiving and giving love
2. Unconditional versus conditional loving of children
3. Affirming versus praising children

1. Children receiving and giving love

HOW CHILDREN FEEL about themselves has a telling effect on all aspects of their lives. Their feelings about themselves determine the friends and partners they will choose, how they will use their aptitudes and abilities, how they will fare educationally and, later on, occupationally. It affects their creativity, integrity and stability, and even whether or not they will be leaders or followers. It is not their genes that determine what they make of their lives but how they see themselves emotionally. Indeed, children's level of self-esteem will greatly influence their sense of fulfilment in life.

Parents are correct to be concerned about how their children will feel about themselves in the future. Children's feelings about self centre on their need to be loved, to love and to be capable of self-love.

Infants are unfairly maligned when they are seen as narcissistic (believing that the world revolves around them). My own experience is that when children reach up to be loved, they also reach out to love. How parents respond to these outstretchings will lead to children seeing themselves either as worthy of being loved or worthy to give love or both. When children are given love and their love is received, they will conclude that they are lovable enough to receive and give love. However, some parents respond to children's need to receive love but not to their need to give love. This creates a major insecurity in children since they will not risk reaching out to love and will cling tenaciously to being loved (half a loaf is better than no loaf!). As adults these children will continue to be unable to give love but will be very strong in their demands to be loved.

The contrary can happen where children's giving of love is received but their need for love is not satisfied. These children miss out on the privilege of being loved and will hold determinedly to giving love.

Stereotyping has resulted in male children being good at receiving love but not good at showing it, and female children being good at giving love but not receiving it. Hence the reason why women tend to be seen more as 'carers' and men as 'takers'. Sadly, both sexes miss out on one or other fundamental aspect of love and will remain insecure in that area of loving until it has been resolved. This difference between the sexes in giving and receiving love can result in considerable relationship difficulties.

It is very confusing for children when one parent responds to their need to be loved and not their need to give love and the other parent does precisely the opposite. Wisely, children will identify with the parent who represents the greatest threat to their security and will become the way that parent wants them to be. It would not be safe to try and satisfy the opposing demands of both parents.

It is vital then that both parents (where there are two) ensure that they respond to their children's need to love and be loved. Where this happens, children will internalise their parents' responses and feel that they are good enough to be loved and to love. This internalisation forms the foundation for their sense of their unique and lovable selves.

2. Unconditional versus conditional loving of children

For love to be truly affirming of children, it has to be unconditional. Unconditional love corresponds to the deepest longing not only of children but of every adult. It is the *sine qua non* of giving and receiving love. When children receive love but are not allowed to give love, they cannot experience both sides of the coin of love. Likewise, when children are expected to give love but are not allowed to expect love for themselves, they are limited to a one-sided experience of loving.

The conditional giving of love is what most children experience in homes, schools and communities. What children learn is that their love is received only when they conform to the expectations of parents (and others) and that any falling short results in a rejection of their giving. This is extremely distressing to children and most of them learn quickly to adapt to the demands of parents in order to hold on to their love being accepted by them. However, the threat of not meeting parents' expectations remains and, depending on the frequency, duration and intensity of the threat, children can vary from being mildly to chronically insecure about their love being received. Moreover, they remain frightened of receiving love. The typical conditions for giving love to parents are:

- be perfect
- be clever
- be helpful
- be good
- be academic
- be top of the class
- be like your father (or mother)
- don't be like your father (or mother)
- don't upset your father (or mother)

SEÁN'S MOTHER IS SLIGHTLY OVER-PROTECTIVE...

    – don't cry
    – don't show anger

Conditional receiving of love by parents results in children feeling that it is not their unique person that parents find worthy but their meeting of the parent's behavioural expectations. These children can become chronic people-pleasers and will go to extremes so that their loving will be received. They do not ask for love to be shown to themselves. They consider that it is only their conforming behaviours that parents consider worth receiving.

Conditionality can also be present for those children who have found it safe to receive love but not to show it. These children are often regarded as being 'spoilt' or overprotected. However, their receiving of love from a parent can be tied to such conditions as:

    – need me
    – be dependent on me
    – never leave me
    – don't do things for yourself
    – be helpless

I'D LIKE TO BE ABLE TO PUT MY FEAR OF FAILURE INTO WORDS... BUT I'M AFRAID I'D MAKE A MESS OF IT!

If these children ever attempt to become independent and self-reliant, they quickly find that love is withdrawn. Just like their counterparts described above, they learn that it is not for themselves that they are loved but for their conformity to parental expectations. Depending on the extent of the parents' dependence, their 'over-protected' children will cleverly learn to stay inept, helpless and lacking in confidence. They do not dare risk showing love to their parents or to others.

Unconditional giving and receiving of love is based on the principle that 'person' and 'behaviour' are separate. The person of each child is unique, an unrepeatable phenomenon, sacred, beautiful, lovable and capable. Nothing can add or take away from a child's person. Behaviour is the means by which children explore the worlds they are in and must never become the measure of the love that is given to them or accepted from them. The person of the child is immutable and when children feel it is their person that makes them worthy of giving and receiving love, they become deeply emotionally secure. Unlike one's 'person', 'behaviour' is volatile, here today and gone tomorrow and offers no solid basis for children's security. Those children who attempt to make their giving of love worthy through proving themselves in their behaviour are always frightened that tomorrow they may fail or fall short. Similarly, those children who conform in their behaviour for the sake of being loved, are constantly fearful of risk-taking or appearing strong. In very clear ways parents need to communicate to their children how wonderful they are in their giving of love and how immensely worthy they are of receiving love. When, as inevitably happens, behaviour becomes the measure of children's giving or receiving love, it is vital that parents resolve the rift in the relationship and bring it back to its unconditional state.

3. Affirming versus praising children

Affirmation is the means by which parents can establish the two-way unconditional relationship with their children. Many parents confuse affirmation with praise. Affirmation is the means of mirroring children's unique and lovable persons. Praise is the means to encourage children's responsible behaviours. When you praise children rather than specific behaviours, children will conclude rightly that their person is only acceptable when they show 'good' behaviour. An example is where a child who has attained good examination results is told 'You're so clever', rather than 'I am pleased with the study efforts you've made and your marks reflect those good efforts'.

To BE HONEST, MUM, I CoULD DO WITH SLIGHTLY LESS UNDIVIDED ATTENTION...

Similarly, when you correct children rather than specific misdemeanours, children assess accurately that it is their person rather than their behaviour that displeases. An example is where a child hits his younger brother and is told 'You're a bad boy', rather than 'I am angry when you hit your brother and I do not want you to do that again'.

My PARENTS SAY I'M OF GREAT WORTH TO THEM ... IN FACT MY TRAINERS ALONE COST OVER EIGHTY QUID!

Children intuitively know when it is only a behaviour that is being corrected or praised and when this is so their sense of person does not become threatened. I am reminded of of a young mother who had begun to correct her conditional way of relating to her four-year-old son and told him one day, with no behavioural strings attached, 'You are very special to me'. He responded with 'And to think I have to do nothing to deserve that'.

The affirmation of the child's person involves certain elements:

The affirmation is a mirror of what every child is
Every child is of worth, lovable, capable, unique and special. To suggest to your child that he is more special than another puts pressure on your child to be 'better' than others and will give him a false sense of self.

The medium of a verbal affirmation is an 'I' message
When a parent tells a child 'You're wonderful', the child may not be convinced of the affirmation because it carries no message about the parent whose regard is so important to her.

It is more accurate and more influential to send an 'I' affirmation: 'I see you as beautiful' or 'I enjoy your wonder' or 'You are special to me'.

The affirmation is sincere and genuine
If a parent is not genuine and sincere about the affirmation and does not really feel that the child deserves it, the parent's non-verbal language (facial expression, tone of voice, body posture, eye-contact) will give him or her away and the affirmation will be rejected as insincere.

The affirmation is given unconditionally
An affirmation is an expression of something a parent feels and perceives in a child and must not be given to gain a particular response (otherwise it is conditional and manipulative). When an affirmation is conditional, children are quick to spot its strategic purpose and will reject the affirming message.

The most powerful affirmation is undivided attention to your child
Avoid effusive compliments, which are rarely sincere and genuine. Silent holding, a hug, a benign look, a reassuring smile, a nod, a touch, are powerful ways to affirm children. Always be sure to give them your full attention.

Spontaneous unconditional affirmations are the most powerful

Focus your affirmation on what is important to your child
Look for signs from your child of what is important to him or her. Parents can be sure that being seen as lovable, capable,

special and unique are important, but other possibilities may include: looks, dress, interests, hobbies, friendships.

Remember that an affirmation values some unique aspect of your child, such as a particular perception of things or a creative way of problem-solving or choice of interests. Praise, on the other hand, focuses on some action, such as tidiness, application to study, obedience, spontaneous helping in the kitchen, doing homework responsibly and so on. It is best to praise the effort in the action rather than the performance of the action.

The important messages children need to hear regarding their worthiness to receive and give love are: 'You are of immense worth and uniquely lovable and your presence or absence matters'. The latter is often overlooked. Children, when they have been away from home or when a parent has been away, need to know not only that they were missed but that their loving was missed. Many adults who were fostered out to aunts or grandparents when they were children, beg to know 'What was wrong with me that I was the one sent away?' Parents, too, need to be aware that their mere physical presence is not sufficient to reassure them of their worth. Children need to be shown in verbal and physical ways that they are loved and that their loving is received. Silent holding, the embrace, the hug, the pat on the back, the warm eye-contact always speak louder than mere verbal statements such as 'I love you' or 'You're so special to me'.

CHAPTER 2: CHILDREN FEELING CAPABLE

1. All children are geniuses!
2. Making learning a positive experience

1. All children are geniuses!

IT COMES AS a complete surprise to many parents to hear that every child (except those who suffer brain damage) is immeasurably capable and intelligent. Science has shown that human beings use only about two per cent of their billions of brain cells. It is grossly inaccurate to label any child as 'slow', 'average', 'dull' or 'bright'. It is accurate to say that each child is a genius. Most children lack confidence because they rarely receive any affirmation of their limitless capacity. This deficit has arisen from a confusion of intelligence with knowledge. It has been assumed that children who are good at certain subjects such as

EVERY CHILD IS A GENIUS... ..SO LONG AS THEIR PARENTS ARE CLEVER ENOUGH TO WORK THAT OUT!

mathematics, English or, nowadays, computers are the clever children and those who show poor performance in these subjects lack intelligence and are 'slow' or 'average' or 'remedial'. In order to survive the home and school cultures, in which they find themselves children necessarily take on the labels inflicted on them; to do anything else would mean risking further hurt and rejection.

A nun who taught in primary school told me a story about a child in her class whom she considered 'not so bright'. Cleverly this child had not approached her during the whole year of class: would you risk contact with someone who had labelled you as 'not so bright?' Surprise of surprises, on the eve of the final day of the school year the child approached the nun and asked her: 'Sister, how would you feel if I brought in some tapes of Madonna tomorrow?' The 'not so bright' child had assessed this nun very well and guessed that Madonna for her would mean the Mother of God. The nun was very honest in her story-telling and told me that when asked the question she began to think 'I wonder what hymns to the Mother of God is the child thinking of playing?' The child caught her hesitancy and moved in quickly with a follow-up request: 'And Sister would it be all right if we had a bit of a dance as well?' The nun replied 'Oh that would be lovely'. The following day the child came in armed with her Madonna and other pop/rock tapes. She cleared the classroom, set it up disco-style, hit the music

MY MUM SAYS I'M GOD'S GIFT..

LET'S HOPE GOD KEPT THE RECEIPT!

and, when she got up to dance, everyone stood in awe of what this child could do with her body. The so-called 'bright children' did not move from their seats. Why were these children not attending a remedial class for the intelligent use of their bodies? Why is it that there are not special classes for children who, for example, have not learned to draw, or socialise, or identify their emotions, or for children who possess domestic skills or understand geography? As long as it is only those children who possess poor knowledge of English or mathematics who are sent to special classes, discrimination will continue to exist in schools and homes, condemning these children to a poor sense of their capability. On the other hand, those children who show high levels of knowledge in these core subjects are condemned to fears of not maintaining high performance standards.

When children internalise messages like 'You're a fool', 'You're slow', 'You're average', they will act in accordance with them. Only when they are convinced of the opposite message, 'You are vastly able', by parents and teachers will they let go of the limiting labels imposed upon them.

What about children who are deemed geniuses or gifted? Do these children condradict the idea that all children are geniuses? Not so! Ninety-seven per cent of children who are labelled 'genius' or 'gifted' make no important social contribution as adults. There is evidence that these so-called 'gifted' persons spend the rest of their adult lives attempting to catch up on deficits in the emotional, social, sexual and spiritual areas of knowledge. These children are not more intelligent than other children but they have worked extremely hard in one or two fields of knowledge, to the detriment of other equally important ones. Usually they have had the benefit of one-to-one teaching and are highly driven to please one or both of their parents.

2. Making learning a positive experience

Children love to learn and have a natural curiosity but these can be extinguished by the way parents and teachers react to children's efforts to learn and to their experiences of failure or success.

The fuel of learning is effort and when children's efforts are encouraged and praised, their endless potential to learn will thrive. However, if adults have unrealistic expectations of children and greet their learning efforts with ridicule and criticism when they do not get it right, children quickly and cleverly find ways of reducing or eliminating further hurt through avoidance, perfectionism or rebelliousness.

Every effort is an attainment. For example, if a child misspells the word animal as annamall he deserves praise most of all for his efforts and then for the letters he formed and for the letters he put together correctly (animal). By recognising what the child has attained and praising him for it, you keep alive the child's love of

learning, and he is now ready for the next challenge of learning to spell the word 'animal'. By putting the correct spelling opposite his effort, you can show him clearly what he has attained and what he has yet to learn.

When adults put the emphasis on performance rather that effort and react harshly to poor performance, they make learning threatening for children in two ways. Firstly, the stern or harsh correction threatens children's prime need to be loved and to love and they will take strong actions to protect that need. Loving must always come before learning. Secondly, expecting children to do things right leads to learning becoming extremely stressful, because the risks of failing and displeasing are very great. In order to eliminate these real risks to their sense of worth, children may ingeniously resort to strategies of avoidance ('with no effort, no failure; with no failure, no rejection'), rebelliousness ('with control of adults' expectations, no failure; with no failure no rejection') and sickness ('when I'm sick, no expectations; with no expectations, no failure'). Another powerful protector that children employ when learning threatens their need to be loved is fear and timidity. When children show such vulnerabilities, adults tend to treat them more gently or with 'kid gloves' – who is controlling whom?

It is a sad indictment of our family, school and work cultures that the most common anxiety experienced by children and adults alike is performance anxiety. Performance anxiety drives children into hating learning or aiming for the average ('I can't fail when I get you to have only average expectations of me') or dropping out of school or compensating in academic knowledge to the detriment of emotional and social development.

Children can also lose their love of learning when parents do not show interest in, nor encourage and praise their efforts to

I'D LIKE TO TALK TO YOU ABOUT THE DANGERS OF AVOIDANCE...

OH MUM— CAN'T WE DO IT LATER?

learn. When parents themselves do not show a love of learning, there is a real danger that children will imitate their apathy.

A powerful means of keeping children's love of learning alive is to help them to embrace failure and success as essential components of learning and not see them as messages about their goodness or worth. If mistakes and failures are greeted with 'put down' messages, ridicule, scolding, comparisons with others or physical punishment, then who in their right mind would want to continue wholeheartedly to pursue learning? Failure is integral to learning; it is the jewel in the crown of learning. Failure provides the important knowledge of what has been attained, of what needs to be corrected, and it provides the stepping-stone to the next step of learning. If, when mistakes occur, children run away, cover up, blame others, get upset, they miss out on learning. Failure must be redeemed as integral to learning and must no longer be an emotional threat to children's self-esteem.

Equally, success must cease to be a reason for affirming and praising children; otherwise they come to believe they are worthy of love only when successful. There are as many children who are fearful of success as there are those who are fearful of failure. To be successful means a lifetime of unrealistic expectations and a high risk of failure. There is also a sizeable number of children who are terrified of not being successful and they put tremendous pressure on themselves to maintain high performance. When they fail they can be suicidal.

The experience of success complements the experience of failure which is a stepping-stone to the learning outcome. Failure and success are the nuts and bolts of learning; to use them to motivate children – 'You're bad when you fail' and 'You're wonderful when you succeed' – destroys children's love of learning. Neither is it wise to use the words as as if they were absolutes. There is no such phenomenon as 'a successful person' or 'a failure'. Our everyday lives are a continual mixture of failures and successes. This pattern is essential to learning. When you praise effort and attainment and avoid using the mechanics of learning to reinforce motivation then children will not lose their eagerness to learn.

Comparisons with others also damage children's love of learning. For example, when a child is told 'You're not as clever as your brother', this undermines the child's academic confidence and may doom him to avoidance of or over-working at school learning. It is necessary for parents to be aware that children within a family will often go opposite ways in the selection of academic subjects and interests. Not only does this reduce the risk, for example, of being compared, it is also a means of establishing a unique identity within the family. Every child has a strong inner drive to establish her own distinct identity and reinforcing their differences will help children to thrive.

Parents would also do well to acknowledge all fields of knowledge as important and not just academic subjects. Too many children are maligned and often inappropriately labelled because of this academic bias in our culture. When parents remove these blinkers, they will see that each child has established high competence in one area or another.

Whether in the academic area or in other fields of learning,

TOMMY FROM DOWN THE ROAD IS LESS AFFECTED BY COMPARISONS THAN YOU ARE...

yet another means of maintaining love of learning is never to praise or correct children. To do so means, as already shown, that children equate their 'goodness' with 'being good' and their 'badness' with 'being bad'. Children are not their behaviour. Praise the behaviour, particularly effort: 'I'm pleased with the effort you put into your school work.' Similarly, correct the behaviour but keep intact your relationship with the child. To say 'You're a bold boy for not doing your homework' blocks a child emotionally as his relationship with you is threatened. It is more accurate to correct the behaviour: 'I'm not happy that your homework is not done and I'm asking you do it now, please'. Affirm the wonder, goodness, uniqueness, lovability and capability of the child, praise all efforts to learn and correct the misdemeanour but never the child.

CHAPTER 3: CHILDREN FEELING UNIQUE

1. Every child is special
2. Children need to be seen for themselves

1. Every child is special

EVERY NEWBORN CHILD is a unique phenomenon in the world and an unrepeatable happening. A powerful way of boosting children's sense of themselves is to tell them genuinely and lovingly 'You are special; one of a kind'. This specialness need to apply also to children's sense of their bodies. Regrettably, many children are compared in physical looks to other children and this can cause them either to feel inferior (for example when told 'Your brother is very handsome') or superior ('You're much more beautiful than your sister'). Critical remarks about and labelling ('fat slob', 'pull-through for a rifle') of body size, shape, skin colour, hair colour, height, weight can leave children extremely shy of mixing with peers and adults for fear of further hurtful experiences. No two children are physically alike

My PARENTS USED To CRITICISE MY SHAPE... BUT NOW THEY'VE SHAPED UP THEMSELVES!

and it is vital that each child is affirmed for his or her unique and wonderful body. Beauty, as defined by Western culture, may be only 'skin deep', but it cuts deep into people's acceptance of their physical selves. It is important to see that it is not only 'put down' messages but also physical comparisons which cause body-image difficulties. I have helped as many people who dread 'losing their looks' as those who hate or dislike their bodies.

Linked to each child being special is the determination of each to fashion his own unique and creative way of living out life. The fewer threats there are to children's sense of their specialness, the more they will create a fulfilling and productive life for self and others. When children have to mask their specialness because of pressure to conform to how parents, teachers and other significant adults perceive them, their creativity, productivity and self-fulfilment will be seriously curtailed.

2. Children need to be seen for themselves
Not only do children have strong needs to feel loved and to feel capable, they also have a need to individualise themselves. This is

why children often go the opposite to each other in terms of how they behave and what knowledge fields and activities attract them. A typical contrast is where one brother is academic and the other sports-oriented. If both were academically motivated, it would be difficult for them to establish distinct identities. It is important that parents and teachers not only observe the ingenuity of the process but also act to reinforce the individual pathways children choose. To go against children's drive to be different in behaviour is a recipe for conflict and is unlikely to change the direction the individual child has chosen. Indeed children will necessarily and rightly 'dig their heels in' and resist adults' attempts to change their behavioural preferences. Comparison in verbal form ('Why aren't you like your brother?') is unwise, causes immense hurt and feelings of rejection and may result in the child losing interest even in preferred activities. Here the child concludes that 'I don't want to be like my brother', 'I'm not seen and respected for being myself', and 'There seems little point in attempting to prove myself'. Avoidance, apathy or half-hearted efforts can be the effects of making comparisons between children. Sometimes you get fierce, hostile and unhealthy competition between children, resulting in extreme pressure on them to be better than one another. Learning then ceases to be pleasurable, and family and classroom problems are likely results.

Parents and teachers who recognise and reward children's attempts to individualise themselves create productive relationships with children. These adults know that where children's motivation lies is where most learning will occur. Forcing children to go against their intuitive life choices is not acceptable and serves only to block or distract from the wonderful potential of children.

CHAPTER 4: HOW PARENTS FEEL ABOUT THEMSELVES

1. Parents who feel nothing for themselves
2. Parents who live for their children
3. Parents who want their children to live their lives for them
4. Parents who love themselves

HOW PARENTS FEEL about themselves can vary along a continuum of 'I feel nothing for myself' to 'I feel deep love for myself'. Parents who feel nothing for themselves are not in an emotional position to parent because they can neither give nor receive love. There are those parents who feel good enough to love but not to be loved and vice versa. Those who feel only good enough to give love will live their lives for their children (and partners) and those who feel only good enough to receive love will expect their children (and partners) to live their lives for them. Parents who have a deep acceptance of themselves and feel free to give and receive love will unconditionally love their children.

1. Parents who feel nothing for themselves
Regrettably there are parents who, when children, were neither loved nor allowed to love. These parents can manifest their despair through addiction to work and material wealth, total lack of emotion, addictions to alcohol or other drugs, violence, physical illness and suicidal behaviours. Another way such parents can manifest their despair is through creating a family where each member has to be the same and outsiders are totally excluded. Incest is not unusual in these families and the children, as adults, have huge difficulties in leaving such families.

When they do manage to leave they dare not return since they are now perceived as outsiders.

The parents in these examples have no sense that their goodness, uniqueness and lovability deserve any response, and it is even too risky for them to show love to or receive love from their children. Not to be loved or allowed to love plunges children and adults into the darkness of loveless lives. The children of loveless parents are at risk not only of not being loved and allowed to love, but also of physical and sexual abuse. These parents have learned to protect themselves through the absolute conviction that nobody could ever see any good in them, not even their own children. Thankfully, the percentage of parents who are like this is small compared to those who can receive love but not give it or those parents who can give love but not receive it. However, it is incumbent on society to detect the children at risk from troubled parenting and set up loving relationships for them; otherwise the whole sad cycle repeats itself.

2. Parents who live for their children

Some parents live for their children, disabling them through doing everything for them. The children of these parents may feel loved but they will not feel safe to return love. Neither do they dare attempt to be independent and self-reliant. But they are allowed to be over-demanding and irresponsible. As adults, the children who conformed to the conditional expectations of this type of parent will either have difficulty in fleeing the nest or will marry a partner who, like their parent, perpetuates their helplessness. Even though married, they will continue to feel obliged to pay regular visits to their over-giving parent.

Children Feeling Good

Children who identify with parents who over-protect become like them. They will believe that they have no importance and will want to live their life for others. Like their parents, these children will manifest behavioural characteristics typical of carers:
- over-pleasing
- non-assertive
- suppression of own needs
- excellent at identifying the needs of others
- avoidance of conflict
- only feeling good enough to show love but not receive it
- difficulty in receiving affection and compliments
- timidity

These children always take their cues from others and are fearful of taking their cues from themselves. They live their lives responding to the needs of others and develop an amazing expertise at helping others. But there is a deep subconscious level of unhappiness owing to their not experiencing being loved, not loving self and not being free to live their own lives. However, to allow these powerful needs to surface would mean risking the loss of what they feel secure in doing – loving others.

Some children rebel against the parent who over-protects, being determined not to be suffocated and controlled. However, their rebelliousness does not breed independence and separateness but an aggression that attempts to counter-control. As adults, they very often subconsciously avoid intimate relationships for fear of being taken over by someone who resembles their parents. They have not the inner security to feel they can remain in charge in the face of adults who attempt to be always there for them. The reason for this poor level of self-control is that they have not

experienced the security of being able to show love and they have become very cautious about receiving love. It is not too difficult to identify these children who may be:
- rebellious
- uncomfortable with emotional closeness
- aggressive
- hostile
- disobedient
- highly susceptible to peer influence

There are other children who respond to the over-nurturing parent by conforming to the need of the parent to give love but not receive it. These children will hold on dearly to the love being given and will, necessarily, become over-demanding, selfish, attention-seeking, helpless and dependent. As adults they will attract persons who will take care of them but they will remain fearful of showing love. Parents who allow this one-sided relationship to occur have a major responsibility to resolve their own limiting feelings about themselves and to free their children to love, receive love, love self and live out their own unique lives without fear.

3. Parents who want their children to live their lives for them

Another possible reaction of parents who do not feel good about themselves is to dominate and control their children into living their lives for them. These parents, like over-protective parents, are highly dependent on what other people think about them. They see their children as extensions of themselves and do everything to ensure that their children do not become a source of embarrassment or ridicule for them. Observe the reactions of many parents when their children 'misbehave' in public or when

My MUM ALWAYS WANTED To JOIN THE CIRCUS...

they are successful. The former behaviour merits withdrawal of love, harsh criticism and ridicule; the latter high praise and adulation. Both responses add to children's insecurity: children who feel they have let their parents down dread doing so again and those who feel they have pleased their parents through success fear not being able to maintain these standards and their parents' approval. The children of parents who manifest their insecurities through dominating, irritable, aggressive and pressurising behaviours live their lives according to the parents' 'shoulds' and 'should nots':

– you should be good
– you should be clever
– you should be obedient
– you should be perfect
– you should be like me
– you should not contradict me
– you should not have ideas of your own
– you should never let me down

Most children conform to parents who are cross, over-demanding and irritable. To rebel would mean risking the loss of being able to give love. There are some children who do rebel and these children are often covertly supported by the parent who is victim of the dominating parent. Indeed, these children's rebelliousness is often motivated by the need to protect the parent who is at the mercy of their over-bearing partner. Unfortunately, children do the opposite of what the dominant parents want and show reluctance to take on responsibilities, aggression, bullying, avoidance of schoolwork, indecisiveness, confusion, lack of direction, poor concentration and little motivation to learn.

Those children who conform at least maintain the experience of giving love but continue to be deprived of the experience of receiving love. Those children who rebel lose out in both the giving and receiving of love from the parent who dominates, but they may have had the privilege of receiving love from the parent who is passive. As adults these children will have difficulty in forming relationships with a person of the same gender as the parent who attempted to over-control them. Regrettably, they will use the same aggressive strategies as their parents in their interpersonal relationships.

Parents who manifest their insecurities through over-controlling behaviours have the responsibility to seek help to resolve their poor feelings about themselves so that their children do not lose out on experiencing full acceptance of themselves and the freedom to love and be loved and to live their own unique lives.

4. Parents who love themselves

Parents who are open to their own goodness, worth, capability, uniqueness and lovability are in a position to mirror the same for their children. I am convinced that babies are well aware of their awesomeness, but when this is not reflected back to them, particularly by parents, they shadow it by taking on the parents' own rejection of themselves.

Parents who unconditionally love themselves love their children, see their children as separate from them, affirm their uniqueness and capability and encourage their children's own unique ways of being in the world. Their expectations of children are realistic and they are positively firm in demanding responsible behaviours and correcting behaviour that threatens the children themselves or others. They do not confuse the child's person with their behaviour and when they do, they apologise. The relationship with their children is always seen as more important than a behavioural issue. This does not mean that they let children slide out of responsibility, but they are firm on the responsibilities without threatening their relationship with their children or the children's relationship with themselves. Their emphasis is always on praising the effort to learn in the context of their loving relationship with their children. They are very aware that each child within the family will find ways to individualise self and will often go directly opposite to a sibling in terms of interests, hobbies, school subject choices, dress sense and style of relating. Self-possessed parents will be eager to detect these differences and encourage their children in those directions. They

will not compare because they perceive an act of comparison as an act of rejection. These parents do not threaten each other's sense of self in the ways they relate to each other. They are vigilant too in observing how other adults and peers relate to their children and will be quick to confront any threat to their children's well-being. Equally, they will not accept their children putting other people's security at risk.

Parents who love themselves continue to challenge themselves in all aspects of living and they offer similar opportunities to their children. When their children take on challenges, they help them to embrace failure and success as mere stepping-stones to further learning. They know that what counts in taking on any challenge is the effort and the experience. From the realisation of their own limitless capability they put their children in touch with their infinite potential. It is from such a solid base of confidence that these parents and their children are widely productive.

The children of parents who love themselves present the following personal profile:
  – giver and receiver of love
  – confident
  – secure
  – assertive
  – responsible
  – can take justified criticism
  – embraces mistakes and failures as opportunities for learning
  – acknowledges competencies and weaknesses
  – kind and caring of others
  – competitive with self, not with others
  – loves life
  – enjoys challenges
  – needs privacy

CHAPTER 5: PARENTS LEARNING TO LOVE THEMSELVES

1. Loving self is unselfish
2. Changing how you feel about yourself

1. Loving self is unselfish

T HE PRIME RESPONSIBILITY of all adults, especially parents, is to learn to love themselves. Many adults consider loving self as selfish but this is a myth that needs to be extinguished. Parents who do not love themselves are not in a position to love anyone and they can seriously threaten their own well-being as well as their children's. Parents who can receive love but not give it are very demanding, controlling, possessive, critical, attention-seeking and react aggressively when their demands to be loved are not met – hardly unselfish behaviours! Equally, parents who can give love but not receive it are conditional in their loving and any attempt to say 'no' to their over-caring can result in sulking, withdrawal, accusations of 'You don't want or need me anymore' and emotional scenes. These reactions are attempts to restore the one-sided nature of the loving relationship and to maintain children's dependence on the parent. Such behaviour is 'selfishly' motivated and results in children feeling helpless, guilty, dependent and enmeshed with their family.

When parents have deep regard for themselves, they can give and receive unconditional love, they are caring, open, fair, firm on responsibilities and help children to become self-reliant and independent. They also help their children to develop their own unique ways of living and they do not project their own ambitions and unfulfilled needs onto children. They give to give, not give to get, as do those parents who can only receive or those who can only give love. Parents who love self are indeed unselfish.

2. Changing how you feel about yourself

Parents who have no sense of their own goodness, worth and capability need psychotherapeutic help to heal their relationships

with themselves and to learn to trust relationships with others, even with their own children. These individuals have become so convinced of their own unworthiness, they cannot believe that even their own children could love them. Regrettably, they project their own hate or dislike of themselves onto the children and react to them in the rejecting ways they treat themselves.

Parents who are good at giving but not receiving love do not tend to emphasise or take responsibility for their own welfare; the needs of others always come first. Equally, parents who can receive love but are poor at giving it attempt to make others responsible for their happiness, and do not entertain the notion that they are responsible for their own lives. Starting-points for both sets of parents for changing how they feel about themselves are:

– affirming their worthiness to both receive and give love
– taking responsibility for their own needs
– establishing a loving relationship with themselves

The relationship with self is a major adult responsibility. This is not a benign issue, because failure by parents to become their own minders means dooming themselves to lives of dependence on each other and on their children, and leads to insecurity, anxiety and a low level of self-fulfilment. Furthermore, the lack of regard for self by parents seriously reduces their effectiveness in rearing children to become self-reliant, confident, secure, responsible and independent. The contrary is also true. Parents who develop a deep regard and responsibility for themselves bring about maturity and security in their children.

A relationship with self involves all the caring behaviours that unconditionally loving parents show to their children:
- affection
- warmth
- nurturing
- belief in one's capability
- acceptance
- affirmation of uniqueness
- praise and encouragement of efforts
- listening
- support
- understanding
- spending time alone
- challenging
- talking positively to
- providing special treats
- positively correcting difficult behaviours
- protecting
- ensuring responsible behaviour
- compassion
- allowing expression of all feelings
- being fair
- being humorous

Adults need to show this range of caring behaviours towards themselves. In doing this, they redeem their loving and capable sense of self and they model how children need to relate to themselves. It is very confusing for children when parents are over-caring of them but careless of themselves. It is equally bewildering when parents are not caring of their children but are over-demanding in their expectations that their children should care for them. Parents who love and take responsibility for themselves are in a wonderful position to see their children as separate from them and to provide the opportunities for them to live out their own unique lives.

The relationship with self needs to be primarily emotional in nature so that all parents' thoughts and actions towards themselves are infused with a loving celebration of self. Love, affirmation, acceptance and caring of self need to be practised daily so that old habits of feeling unworthy, lack of confidence, avoidance of challenges, aggression or passivity and neglect of physical well-being are healed.

Parents' feelings about themselves will gradually change when all actions towards themselves (and others) are of a self-loving and caring nature, whether these have to do with domestic responsibilities, work, leisure, diet, physical exercise, life-style, spirituality, friendships, study and so on.

YOU'RE THE ONE WHO TOLD DAD HE NEEDED TO GET A BALANCED LIFESTYLE!

Some examples are given below:
- affirm your worthiness to give and receive love
- value and unconditionally love self
- accept self
- do activities in a calm and relaxed way
- eat healthy foods
- give yourself adequate time to eat and digest
- listen to self
- determine your own needs
- take responsibility for meeting your needs
- encourage yourself to do your best
- embrace failures as opportunities for learning
- be assertive about your beliefs
- be spontaneous and open
- follow your own ideas, beliefs and convictions
- take time and space for self
- take regular physical exercise
- develop a balanced lifestyle
- treat self
- challenge self

Changing how parents feel about themselves is a lifetime process and requires consistent practice. It is only through persistent caring of themselves that the old, painful and limiting ways will be extinguished. The fruits of change are: security, independence, freedom to be self, spontaneity, unconditionality with self and others, openness to change, assertiveness, peacefulness, increased potential for self-fulfilment and effective parenting. It is primarily through their relationship with themselves that parents can be guaranteed that their children will grow up feeling good about themselves.

CHAPTER 6: HELPING TROUBLED CHILDREN

1. Parents are not the only minders
2. Signs indicating distress
3. Restoring the loss of loving

1. Parents are not the only minders

THERE IS NO doubt that parents are the major players in the development of how children feel about themselves. However, it would be unwise not to be vigilant about other significant people in children's life – grandparents, child-minders, teachers, aunts and uncles, neighbours and peers. An uncharted area is the emotional and social effects siblings have on each other. Generally speaking, effective parents are automatically watchful of how others interact with their children and vice versa.

Nevertheless, hidden neglect can slip by some parents. Certainly, the influence of child-minders must be more closely looked at, particularly during the formative period from birth to five years. Very often child-minders see more of the children than do working parents. Careful selection of a child-minder is an important responsibility for parents who stay in employment outside the home. Observation is the most reliable assessment tool; while qualifications provide some guarantee, they do not ensure effective and loving caring. Neither is the experience of having already reared a family a reliable criterion since you would need a looking-glass into the past to evaluate how effective was the parenting. Spending time in joint-parenting with a child-minder is the best way to select a carer for children. This observation needs to be ongoing, particularly when you collect the children from the minder.

Always enquire how the day went and watch for discrepancies between what is said and what is conveyed non-verbally. A child-minder who says 'Everything was fine' but whose eye-contact, facial expression, body-posture and tone of voice suggests something is awry, needs to be further questioned (not interrogated!). It is important that child-minders feel that it is emotionally safe to voice difficulties to parents. Emphasis by parents on the partnership in parenting involved is helpful. Acknowledgment too that minding children is not an easy profession, and that difficulties are likely to emerge which will need to be jointly problem-solved, will ease difficulties child-minders may have in declaring problems

2. Signs indicating distress
No matter who or what is the source of children not feeling good, it is important that parents recognise the signs of distress

and immediately take remedial action. Children can manifest their insecurities physically, emotionally, socially, intellectually, sexually or behaviourally, or present signs across a number or all of these media. The most common of these symptoms are given below:

Physical signs
Nail-biting, bed-wetting, soiling, abdominal pain, facial grimacing, rapid eye-blink, poor appetite, frequent complaints of headaches.

Emotional signs
Feeling easily hurt, hypersensitivity to criticism, clinging behaviour, overexcitability, extravagant emotional expression, frequent nightmares, hostile reactions to positive correction,

extreme shyness, lack of confidence, homesickness, high anxiety, timidity, fear of new challenges, worrying unduly, frequent day-dreaming, frequently looking sad, undue distress over failures and mistakes.

Social signs

Frequent requests for help, attention-seeking, argumentative, disruptive of other people's activities, complaining of unfair treatment, resentment of parent, isolating self from others, avoiding games, complaining of 'not feeling loved' or looking for reassurance of being loved, little or no eye contact, extreme nervousness when answering questions, wanting to please all the time, few or no friends.

Intellectual signs

Over-studious, poor motivation to learn, appears 'lost in another world', obsessional and/or compulsive behaviours, over-absorption in hobby, schoolwork or interests, failure to respond when spoken to, mental blocks when either answering questions or doing an examination.

Sexual signs

Frequent relaying of sexual stories, excessive self-stimulation, over-interest in sexual matters, over-modest, hostile reaction to genuine hug.

Behavioural signs

Hyperactivity, speaking too fast, destructiveness of property, aggressive, frequent minor delinquencies, not listening, blaming others, showing-off, bullying, dominating younger siblings, being passive, being over-exact, avoiding schoolwork, frequently absent from home, rarely going out.

Children's feelings about themselves are peculiar to the relationships they have with the significant people in their lives and need to be understood and responded to within these relationships. No matter what the source of or manifestation of children's insecurities, something needs to be done to change how they are feeling about themselves. Detecting the signs of distress is only the first step in helping children feel that they are worthy of receiving and giving love.

3. Restoring the loss of loving

A fundamental aspect of helping distressed children to understand that their troubled behaviour is not designed to make life difficult for parents but rather to alert parents to their distress. When parents react aggressively or passively to any of the signs of distress listed above, they will not be successful in helping troubled children. Such responses serve only to make

things go from bad to worse. If parents feel they are going to lose control, it is best that they quickly remove themselves from the child. If parents react passively to signs of children's inner conflicts, they need to find ways of empowering themselves so that they can be more fully there for their children.

Staying separate from and being compassionate towards and understanding of distressing behaviours is fundamental to healing children's inner turmoil. With that in place, parents need next to discover the causes of children's distress so that healing actions can be initiated. The cause may be their own relationship with the child or the relationship between the child and somebody else such as child-minder, teacher, peer, sibling. Patience is needed in this quest since children may not immediately reveal the cause because of fear of judgement or appearing weak or becaue of the risk of further neglect. Children must be reassured that they are loved and that they will be listened to when they are ready to talk. All the time parents need to look at how they generally interact with the child who is presenting the problem. Whether or not they know the causes, they must immediately and persistently behave in ways that help the child to feel good about self. This involves engaging in all those loving actions that reassure children about their lovability and capability.

When, in spite of parents' best efforts, children continue to be distressed, professional help may need to be sought. The professional of choice is a clinical psychologist, family therapist, psychotherapist or counsellor who has an in-depth knowledge of children, family dynamics and who has experience of helping children and families in distress. General medical practitioners can recommend reliable practitioners, but direct contact with these professionals can also be made by the parents. Do not be fearful of asking the professional contacted about his or her experience in helping children with the presenting problems. Persist in seeking help until the child returns to feeling good about self.

OTHER TITLES BY TONY HUMPHREYS

Books

A Different Kind of Teacher
Self-Esteem: The Key to Your Child's Education
The Family: Love It and Leave It
The Power of 'Negative' Thinking
Myself, My Partner
A Different Kind of Discipline

Spoken-Word Audio Cassettes

Self-Esteem for Adults
Self-Esteem for Children
Embrace Failure